For Alessandra, Geneva, and Devon,
the star, moon, and the sun of my life.

Text copyright © 2021 by John S. LoConte, Ph.D.

youngzenminds.com

All rights reserved. This book, or parts thereof, may not be reproduced, transmitted, or stored in an information retrieval system in any form or by any means, graphic, electronic, or mechanical, including photocopying, taping, and recording, without prior written permission from the publisher.

ISBN 978-0-578-86952-0

First printing 2021

Illustrations and cover art by Kathrine Gutkovskiy

Cover design by Kathrine Gutkovskiy and Jodi Giddings
Interior design by Jodi Giddings

ZACK NATURALLY
A Child's Zen Companion

JOHN S. LOCONTE, PH.D.
art by Kathrine Gutkovskiy

They say it happens every day.
A child somewhere comes home
   to say,
"I hate my life, and I hate me.
   I'm not the way I want to be."

"What happened, son?"
   Mom wiped Zack's tears.

"It's school," snapped Zack.
   "They tease me there."

"Maybe I didn't smile enough.
 Maybe I should have acted more tough.
 I'm small and slow. My hair is red and poofy.
 Kids stare at my big ears. Mom, I look so goofy."

"Oh boy," replied Mom. "I wish you could see,
 How people love you, Zack, naturally."

"Son, your thoughts about you are so unkind.
You're stuck in the little, dark room of your mind.
You think the kids hate you? Do you know if it's true?
You're at a new school, and it's only day two!"

"But my thoughts are true, Mom.
They came from my head."

Mom shrugged her shoulders, smiled wisely, and said,
"Zack, many of our thoughts are mistaken, of course.
Remember you thought you could ride a seahorse?
And your silly thoughts about my plants in the sink?
You asked, "Mom, without lips, how can plants drink?"

"Zack, neither sloths nor snails, rivers nor brooks,
Care how they run or fear how they look.
A fox would never trade his red hair for brown.
And an elephant's ears don't make her frown.
You love your pup, Bud, though he is quite small.
And Shelly, your turtle,
moves hardly at all."

"If you're not feeling right, it's your thoughts that are wrong. Our thoughts leave us out. In life we belong."

"Mom, you're not listening. I'm talking about me! When I look in the mirror I don't like what I see."

"But, Zack," replied Mom, "your eyes must be blinking. The mirror's not you. It just shows what you're thinking."

"Remember the funhouse
   on the boardwalk last May?
Those trick mirrors changed you every which way!
Looking in mirrors makes us feel small.
Looking out windows connects us to all.
You think that there's something
   wrong about you?
I'll ask you some questions.
   You might change your view."

"Zack, does the sun feel embarrassed for shining too bright?
Does darkness feel bad for creating the night?
Do planets feel awkward for taking up space?
Is the Earth a big loser for taking third place?"

"No, I'm the big loser," replied Zack as he winced.

"Zack, your mind's in the clouds.
    You're hard to convince!"

"Zack, do falling stars fear that the heavens will laugh?
Is the moon not enough when it shows only half?"

"Mom, falling stars sparkle like the Fourth of July!
And half-moons turn whole again. They never cry."

"Zack, does a tree feel sad when its leaves drop in fall?
Or when its limbs break off in a heavy snow squall?
Does its wood wish it wouldn't when it gives us a splinter?
No. A tree regrets nothing from spring until winter."

"Mom, the kids still don't like me. I know that for real.
But ask me more questions. They help how I feel."

"Should clouds go to jail when they steal the sky's blue?
And when rain falls on picnics, what else can rain do?
Are earthquakes at fault when they make the ground shake?
And when ice melts to water, did it make a mistake?
We don't judge water when it overflows creeks.
And I won't judge your tears, because those are your cheeks."

"Zack, we don't laugh at water for not staying in shape.
Nor put wind in its place with glue or with tape.
The setting sun always sinks really low,
Yet wakes us each morning to get up and go."

"Oh, Mom, it's silly to tell the sun not to sink!
And water just runs. It doesn't care what we think."

"Zack, there are cheetahs that run as fast as the light.
And snails that crawl in slow-motion delight.
The world is one big, magical puzzle.
Every size, shape, and color fits without trouble."

"Did you know there are zebras with no stripes to claim?
And boy ladybugs who aren't bugged by their name?"

"So your hair is red, Zack. It's kissed by the sun. In your mind that's a problem. In the big world, there's none.
And the legs you describe as so little and slow? They take you everywhere you want to go."

"And your ears that you say are a terrible sight?
You mean the ones that bring you sweet music each night?
And speaking of ears, that's the doorbell's loud sound.
Bud's barking like crazy. Can you see who's around?"

"Sure, Mom, I'll get it. Hey, Bud, it's okay!
I guess, like me, you're cranky today.
Wow, pup, even our ears look the same.
And you have my red hair, but you don't complain.
With your short little legs, you run slowly like me.
How else can I catch up to you naturally?"

"Bud, I'm sure it's the mailman. You have to calm down.
I'll take you out later and walk you downtown.
Maybe Mom's right. Getting outside is the trick.
All **you** need to be happy is grass and a stick!"

"So hang with me, pup.
I want you to stay.
When I feel alone, you wag
bad thoughts away.
You made friends
at the dog park.
I know that it's true.
Maybe some kids will make
friends with me too."

"Hey, Mom! Can I go
    out with my friends?
My bad thoughts really
    fooled me again."

"Sure," replied Mom,
    with the happiest smile.
"Go have a good time.
    See you back in a while."

Mom watched as Zack
    and his friends became one.
This boy without mean thoughts?
    Now **that** was her son!
Who would YOU be
    without YOUR mean thoughts?
The beautiful child you almost forgot.
When YOU'VE had a bad day,
    and your closed mind can't see,
Open your heart like Zack, naturally.

Made in the USA
Las Vegas, NV
18 May 2021